I Found Me

COREY HALL

Copyright © 2018 Corey Hall

All rights reserved. In accordance with U.S. Copyright Act of 1976, the scanning, uploading, and electronic sharing of any part of this book without permission of the publisher constitute unlawful piracy and theft of the author's intellectual property. No part of this book may be reproduced in any form by any electronic or mechanical means (including photocopying, recording or information storage and retrieval) without permission in writing from the author or publisher. Thank you for your support of the author's rights. If you would like to purchase bulk or wholesale copies, please contact the publisher at richterpublishing@icloud.com.

Published by Richter Publishing LLC
www.richterpublishing.com

Book Cover Layout: Richter Publishing

Book Cover Front Image:@sifegrafix & @tchandlerphotography

Editors: Monica San Nicolas & Margarita Martinez

Proofreaders: Homer Allen Samuels, Jr. & Marisa Beetz

ISBN-13: 978-1-945812-63-7

DISCLAIMER

This book is designed to provide information on Bipolar Disorder only. This information is provided and sold with the knowledge that the publisher and author do not offer any legal or medical advice. In the case of a need for any such expertise, consult with the appropriate professional. This book does not contain all information available on the subject. This book has not been created to be specific to any individual people or organization's situation or needs. Reasonable efforts have been made to make this book as accurate as possible. However, there may be typographical and or content errors. Therefore, this book should serve only as a general guide. This book contains information that might be dated or erroneous and is intended only to educate and entertain. The author and publisher shall have no liability or responsibility to any person or entity regarding any loss or damage incurred, or alleged to have incurred, directly or indirectly, by the information contained in this book or as a result of anyone acting or failing to act upon the information in this book. You hereby agree never to sue and to hold the author and publisher harmless from any and all claims arising out of the information contained in this book. You hereby agree to be bound by this disclaimer, covenant not to sue and release. You may return this book within the guarantee time period for a full refund. In the interest of full disclosure, this book contains affiliate links that might pay the author or publisher a commission upon any purchase from the company. While the author and publisher take no responsibility for any virus or technical issues that could be caused by such links, the business practices of these companies and or the performance of any product or service, the author or publisher has used the product or service and makes a recommendation in good faith based on that experience. All characters appearing in this work are fictitious. Any resemblance to real persons, living or dead, is purely coincidental. The opinions and stories in this book are the views of the author and not that of the publisher.

DEDICATION

I dedicate my book to my son, mother, my Uncle Butch, Alonzo Lewis, and anyone else who's been cheated by life.

CONTENTS

DEDICATION v
INTRODUCTION iii
Chapter 1: EARLY LIFE 1
Chapter 2: COLLEGE LIFE 16
Chapter 3: MILITARY LIFE 28
Chapter 4: STRUGGLES IN THE MILITARY 38
Chapter 5: PRISON AND COCAINE 50
Chapter 6: LIFE AFTER THE MILITARY 60
Chapter 7: LIFE AFTER REHAB 73
EPILOGUE: ABOUT BIPOLAR DISORDER 79
ABOUT THE AUTHOR 88

MY SON WILL KNOW I WAS NOT DEFINED BY A DISABILITY.

INTRODUCTION

I wrote this book for my son. I want to show him what it takes to be a man and what steps are necessary for him to be successful in life.

My life wasn't a cake walk growing up. I had many struggles, but the one that affected me the most was an invisible enemy: bipolar disorder.

Through my stories here within my memoir, I want to shed light to the masses about addiction, depression, suicide, and other mental health issues that go along with this illness. At times life is hard, but people living with these conditions have a bigger obstacle to overcome. However, that doesn't mean that we should be cast aside and forgotten about. We first must learn to accept that although we might be different, we can still live a prosperous life if given the right tools.

Ask for help; you do not have to suffer alone. Perfection is unattainable, but I'm okay with not being perfect for the simple fact that every day, I get another opportunity to build on yesterday.

CHAPTER 1
EARLY LIFE

I was born in Stoughton, Massachusetts, and grew up between two cities, Brockton and Taunton. Growing up in Massachusetts, I had a wonderful childhood as one of five siblings. I have one sister who lives in Boston and two half-sisters who live in Texas.

My only brother, Marion Hall (better known as "Pooch"), was essentially my other half. He now lives in Los Angeles. I don't get to see him as much nowadays because he's busy being a successful actor.

Growing up, my brother Pooch and I did everything together. As younger brothers do, I mimicked everything he did. If he played football, I played football. Whatever he picked up, I followed right behind him.

Baseball was a sport I enjoyed. However, Pooch went into boxing and ended up winning the Southern New England Golden Gloves award in 1994. Boxing was the next logical step for him because my father was a trainer at Petronelli Gym out of Brockton, Massachusetts. From my understanding, Goodie and Pat Petronelli were Marvin's trainer and manager. The middleweight champion of the world, Marvelous Marvin Hagler. And my father trained my brother and other fighters.

I would cry when my brother got punched. I always yelled out, "Don't hit my brother!" That was the kind of relationship we had. We fiercely protected one another and were both sports-oriented. My brother also had his nose buried in his schoolwork. Since I looked up to him so much, I followed in his footsteps and enjoyed school when I was younger as well.

As a kid, I always noticed there was a rift between my parents. They fought all the time, mostly over my mother's drinking habits. I didn't even know what "drinking" meant at that young age. All I saw was how much my father disliked it. Around age 10, I came to find out that her drinking was the cause of their divorce. This caused me to have negative feelings toward her. I was angry and confused; I wanted to place blame on her, but I felt conflicted because she was my mother. How could I be hostile toward the woman who gave birth to me?

Years later as an adult, I confronted my mother about her drinking. She clarified that alcohol was a coping mechanism; she'd never felt good enough for my very strict father. As a military man, he demanded a lot from his family. His expectations were set high from the start—it was his way or the highway—and my mom could not deal with failure.

I FOUND ME

One year, my father decided it was best for our family to become Jehovah's Witnesses. Until that point, I was raised Baptist. I never understood his decision, and he never explained. As the man of the house, we did whatever he said, which meant that birthdays and Christmas celebrations disappeared. Looking back, I'd thought at the time that losing those traditions would bother me. I figured I couldn't be a normal child without them. The truth was, I enjoyed spending more time with my brother, no matter what the activity. Having him in my life made me feel numb to losing birthdays and Christmas. To this day, I'm not terribly excited when it comes to celebrating birthdays, at least not with my own.

Throughout elementary school, life was good and ran smoothly. During the spring before middle school, in 1990, my life came to a screeching halt. That warm spring day, Friday the 13th, changed everything. As my friends and I wrapped up our pickup baseball game, I headed home to face a frightening reality. A sea of police cars sat parked in front of my house and blocked off the entire street. As I approached our street, my heart dropped into my stomach. All the flashing lights were around my house.

Thoughts started to race through my mind. Did Dad have a stroke? Did someone die? Was there a break-in? I ran up to the house, but the cops held me back. I kept yelling at them to let me through, but it fell on deaf ears. As I stood there, imagining the worst, my father came out, followed by my brother—both in handcuffs. My heart dropped into my stomach. I knew Dad had a bad temper, but I never imagined he would be arrested. But why my brother? He was my hero; there was no way he could have done anything wrong. What was going on, why wouldn't anyone tell me!? My anger then turned to sorrow. Would I ever see them again? Tears streamed down my face. The thought of losing the two important male role models in my life was too much to bear at my young age.

My parents had already divorced by this time and my father was dating a woman I didn't care for, who was still in the house during the chaos. Moments later, my mother pulled up—and my mother never showed up anywhere unannounced. I knew this was serious.

To this day, I've never formally sat down and discussed my brother's side of the story. However, I've heard the official story a million times, and it changes each time. I will tell you the patchwork version I know today.

At that time, my brother, who was about 16, worked at the local supermarket. Allegedly, he'd said "Hi, sexy," to the girlfriend of a much older employee. The employee followed my brother to the break room and threw some jabs and right hooks. Using his boxing abilities, my brother warded him off and bought enough time to run away safely to our house. He told our father about the events that transpired and Dad's anger boiled over. He was protective of all the neighborhood kids, especially his own. He grabbed his gun and drove to the supermarket with my brother in tow.

They barged into the supermarket during the middle of the day, while the store was packed with busy shoppers. My father carried his .357 chrome magnum through the crowded aisles, his face filled with rage. My brother saw the guy who'd punched him in the back of the store and ran up to him, took a knife from his back pocket that he got from home and stabbed him in the side. When my father finally caught up with them, he opened fire. He fired a shot and missed his target. Ironically, the bullet instead hit the girl my brother had said "Hi, sexy" to. From my understanding, as a result of the wound, she lost her arm and then sued my father. At the time, Dad had a solid job working as a heavy-duty equipment operator for the Big Dig in Boston. After the lawsuit, we lost everything.

My brother was sent to a youth detention center, while my father was sentenced to approximately five years in prison. Because I lived with my father and brother at the time, their sentences immediately became my sentence too. It tore me apart. I didn't want to leave and move somewhere else. They were the two stable things in my life and they couldn't be there for me. This was a big rift for me; I didn't know how to cope. What was I going to do without my big brother and pops?

I was given the choice to move in with my mother, but I didn't want to live with her. Her drinking was really bad and she was unstable. I didn't know at the time that she was an alcoholic trying to deal with what I believe to be a bipolar disorder. Even as a kid, I just knew it was something I didn't want to be around.

I decided instead to move to Melbourne, Florida, to live with my aunt. Instead of moving to be with my mother, I chose to live with a woman I'd never met. It wasn't the worst experience, nor was it the ideal solution. I felt indifferent at first, mostly from absorbing the aftershock of trauma. When you're young, stressful events don't always manifest themselves from day one. You just deal with it because that is what you have to do.

When it came to leaving Brockton—my hometown—it bothered me. I did not want to leave my friends or the place I grew up. Change was difficult for me and I became really depressed. But I had no choice. I was not going to be homeless and I did not want to move in with my mother. I could not deal with her drinking. Little did I know, she was just self-medicating a disease that would soon manifest inside myself.

I remember the first time I saw my aunt. I was convinced my father had broken out of prison and thrown on a wig. Aside from their differing hairstyles, they could have been identical twins. Every feature he had, she shared with him—same height, same build; their eye color was exact to the shade.

I hoped I could pick up the pieces in Florida by jumping back into sports. Doing something familiar could keep me grounded; I wanted to become busy to keep my mind off my father and brother.

I loved living in Florida. Something about the warm air, salt breeze, and palm trees swaying in the wind makes you forget about the past. I made friends easily and all seemed right in the world, if only for a bit.

But the move down the East Coast did not last as long as I wanted. Before my seventh grade year, my mom decided she wanted me back home. My brother was out of the detention center and was now living with her, so she wanted us to be a family again. But I did not want to move; I had really fit in at my new home and was about to start school in Florida. My aunt insisted that I go home, and we got into multiple arguments over it. I cried and begged to stay. No one understood where I was coming from; no one knew what these upsets did to me emotionally. No sixth grader could possibly grasp the issues that arise from excessive drinking. I was no exception.

However, I vividly recalled the mood swings that erupted as a result of my mom's drinking. While I didn't want to move, because I knew what enduring my mom's behavior was like firsthand, I did want to see my brother again and hoped that maybe her situation had improved with him being there. So, I packed my stuff up and off to Boston I went.

I arrived at Logan International Airport to find my mother and brother waiting to pick me up. The cold, dry Boston air was a shock to my system. My body had quickly adjusted to the humidity of the south. While we drove from the airport to the neighborhood where they now lived, I gazed out the windows, missing the palm trees already. She pulled up to a condo complex and parked the car. Somehow, she was able to purchase a condominium in Taunton.

Seeing my mother was rough at first. I didn't speak a word about our past. We kept our conversations short and sweet, like small talk. After all, I wasn't sure what I was really feeling being younger, caught in the middle of such drama. But I just brushed it off because I was excited to see my big bro! I had missed him so much while he was away.

When I entered the new condo, I ran straight to his room. It was pretty sick. He had it all decked out with lots of black lights. Centered against the biggest wall was a large TV, hooked up for the latest video games. Mortal Kombat had just been released on Super Nintendo. We played that all night and day. I was exceptional at those video games and never broke focus. My brother never beat me. After playing even one round, I felt a surge of joy flow through me, like the good 'ol days. It was a great feeling to hang out with him again.

All in all, it seemed things might be okay. It was great to be back with my brother. However, the community where my mom had bought the condo was a mainly Portuguese neighborhood. The kids in the neighborhood spoke a lot of Portuguese around me. To make things worse, there was not a single black person or family amongst us. I didn't know anything about their culture, their language, or their food. I liked it, but it was different from the norm. I couldn't relate to them at all, which was difficult. It was hard to make any friends because we didn't fit in at first.

Being in another new area so quickly forced me to reflect on a place of happiness for comfort. I started missing Florida. I became depressed and had no desire to do anything. I would go to school, then come home and sleep for hours. My brother constantly urged me, "Yo, get up and do something!" But I refused. I had zero energy.

Eventually, my situation reached a low point where I stopped eating all together. My father was still in jail, which didn't help the issue. I know he had done a bad crime, but I still missed having him around. My mom phoned my sister in Texas out of concern. She said, "I can't get this kid to eat nothing." My sister simply replied, "When he gets hungry, he'll eat."

Even so, my mom kept trying to feed me. She cooked all types of food, but I would not touch anything. It wasn't a matter of depression, it was a sign of protest. I refused her cooking because I didn't want her to have the satisfaction of feeding me. The only time I broke my hunger strike was for lunch at school. I don't even remember how I snapped out of that funk. I just did not want to be there. My mom tried her best, I will admit. Still, I didn't want anything to do with her or the family situation.

Over time, I hung around the neighborhood kids and I picked up their culture and customs. I started speaking Portuguese. I even got a job working at a local video store, which was owned by Big Ed, the father of one of the neighborhood kids. At this point, I attached myself to some minor enjoyment with new friends. My main goal was to pass time until my father was released from prison.

One day in that passing time, my brother told me about the upcoming football tryouts. I was hesitant to go at first, but after much persuasion, I agreed. To my luck, I got on the team. Looking back, it was probably the best thing I could have done at that time. Football helped me mentally and physically deal with the tough times I was enduring.

The first few days of practice focused mainly on conditioning. I had lots of pent-up anger and wanted to release it on the field. When I played football as a young kid, my father was my coach. I always wanted to make him proud. And now, since my father was incarcerated, I turned to my brother. Pushing myself to make him proud was a tremendous step forward. I became very motivated and started winning awards. People everywhere suddenly knew my name.

When I made it to high school, Coach Bobby Lane took a strong liking to me. Even though most of the players disliked him for his strict coaching style, I respected him. He reminded me of a white version of my father because he didn't take shit from anybody. Coach Lane taught us all how to problem-solve. He was there for us, he had compassion, and he was very smart. Coach started calling me "Corey Be the God." He told me I was going to be special one day—and I believed him.

In addition to football being a positive outlet in my life, school ran smoothly as well. My teachers, Mrs. George, Mrs. DeSousa, Mrs. Charves, and Matt Mattos loved me and my grades were solid, except for math. Math was a hard subject for me to navigate. However, I had great tutors. My favorite subjects were the major sciences—biology, anatomy, and chemistry—in addition to creative writing. I loved being in the lab, discovering new things about our world. I even took Portuguese as my second language.

Despite loving school, my home life was deteriorating, especially my relationship with my mother. She was a functioning alcoholic and somehow always managed to keep a good job. Unfortunately, her drinking escalated once again. My brother was often out, busy with work and doing his own thing. I kept to myself whenever I was at home to avoid her drunken episodes.

Football was the key. By putting all my focus and energy into football, both as a distraction and enjoyment, I quickly noticed I was undersized compared to other guys on the team. My brother and the coaches preached to me that I needed to start weight training if I wanted to become an elite football player. I wanted to make them all proud, so I hit the weight room and went H.A.M. (hard as a motherfucker). Coach Lane took time with me to ensure I performed the right exercises and lifts.

Soon, I noticed I could move players with increasing ease due to my weight training. When we executed drills at practice, they were no longer a challenge. I was asked to play varsity for the Thanksgiving game, which was a big deal since sophomores didn't play varsity. Coach Matt Mattos would come to me and say, "Corey Hall, it's your time."

Playing on the football team gave me the discipline I needed and my depression and mood were not a problem anymore. It built my self-esteem and really gave me a purpose in life again.

As I started my junior year of high school, my father was released from prison. It was a continental shift, to say the least. It was good to be with my father again, but prison changes people. The day he walked free was the biggest breath of fresh air I ever took in my life. I saw him after a football practice and almost collapsed. I knew it was him, but seeing him in person was like a mirage. I wasn't sure if the sun was playing tricks on my eyes.

In the middle of our hug, I choked up right after he choked up. It was a beautiful and bittersweet moment that's hard to put into words unless you've stood in either of our shoes.

After my father was released, he moved back to Taunton, Massachusetts, where I was living with my mother. I didn't realize at the time that his girlfriend would be moving with him. The problem was that I couldn't stand her. Thankfully, when my father worked for the Big Dig before going to prison, he was affiliated with a union that allowed him to return to work on his release five years later. Resuming his job gave him the opportunity to earn income, which helped him rebuild his life and provide for us again while we were still in school.

My father was still top dawg, but I was mature enough to realize things weren't as clean-cut as I'd always believed. I grew up and comprehended that my hero was human, like me. He was my father, who wore the same kind of clothes I did—not a cape. Before long at Dad's new apartment, my brother moved out to attend the University of Dartmouth. Then, it was just me.

In the midst of all this, I started receiving college recruitment letters for football. I had my heart set on playing at Boston College. I was on the phone back and forth with the coaches. I was told I could walk on because they had just given out one of their last scholarships to Mark Colombo, who played for our rival and later for the Dallas Cowboys. That was understandable because the kid was a beast. Playing at B.C. would have been the only way that I would have stayed in Mass. I decided after seeing my second letter that I would return to Florida. The winters at home were beyond brutal, and honestly, in my opinion, the best football took place in Florida, anyway. I had my dad's entire side of the family living in Florida, which made the decision that much easier.

Football was my ticket to a warmer climate and happier life. With the decision to leave Massachusetts, I adopted a mindset I call "ball owt." I had no regard for my body whatsoever to the point that I would get a concussion, then I'd want to get up and return to the huddle. My trainer at high school at the time, Kris

I FOUND ME

H., would stop me from breaking my limits or my bones. She basically kept me together throughout my football career.

I played on both the JV and varsity teams, which helped improve my skills tremendously. My father and brother came to every one of my football games, and I loved them for it. My mother also showed up to watch me play. Seeing her there gave me an ambiguous feeling. Her support encouraged me, but it didn't change our past. Deep down, I enjoyed seeing her in the stands and was happy she was there. I wondered if it was her way to make amends without actually saying the words face-to-face.

My brother was always funny and was the announcer at a few of my games; therefore, everyone knew him, too. During my senior year, I was voted "Class King." Everyone knew the Hall brothers.

Being good at football made me popular in school, but I never paid attention to achievements like that. I was the guy who always looked out for others who were victims of bullying; I stuck up for them. In high school, bullying was a frequent occurrence. I almost got in a fistfight with a senior who bullied a sophomore in my class. Luckily, Coach Mattos walked toward us in that moment and the senior brushed it off to avoid trouble of his own. Mattos always looked out for me. He turned to me and said, "We need you on the field, Hall."

I had fun in my remaining school years, but I was focused on the bigger picture: playing college football. I worked as hard as I could to receive a scholarship to play in Florida, where my heart remained. At the time, Florida had the best football programs in the nation in my opinion. I always heard about Florida State—F.S.U., The University of Miami—The U, and University of Florida—U.F.

My father always talked about moving back home to Florida, which only added more incentive. My father had left home when he was 17 to join the military and had not been back since. I did have a backup plan, which I kept to myself. I decided if I couldn't play in Florida, my second choice would be joining the armed forces.

In all my enthusiasm, more bad news came my way. I learned that my SAT scores were not high enough for me to be given a scholarship. Even though I'd achieved really good grades, honors classes were weighted differently and counted more than standard classes. Without any honors classes on my transcript, I would have to get an 1100 or better on my SATs in order to be eligible to play college football.

With that information, I sought out my guidance counselor and asked to sign up for higher-level classes. Then, I came into a speed bump of my own. Attending higher-level classes meant there was a bunch of paperwork that I needed to fill out and have my parents' signatures. Because of our poor relationship, I forged my mother's signature. I knew I could do the work for those advanced and honors classes as long as I put my mind to it; and that was exactly what I did. Because of the extra work I did with my tutors, I knew the transition would be seamless.

I FOUND ME

CHAPTER 2
COLLEGE LIFE

As it came time to make my college decision, I really wanted Florida State or The University of Miami (The U), but I also considered Boston University because of its outstanding medical program. B.U. was mainly a school known for hockey, but they still had a football program. I initially wanted to explore biology, specifically herpetology, which is the study of reptiles and amphibians, or DNA research.

I went on a trip to Boston University and came into a bunch of interesting doctors from Massachusetts General. Seeing them firsthand pushed me toward applying; that is, until they cut their football program. That was the end of Boston University.

Before I left for college, my brother continually encouraged me to come down to Florida to show them who I was and to make a name for myself. When I did finally go, I got a taste of their college football firsthand and saw how they trained. I noticed their work ethic did not rival mine, and I knew I could compete at a higher level. My mindset boiled down to the assumption that by playing Division I football, I would automatically get a tryout for the NFL. That was the plan.

One day not long after my trip, a childhood friend, Don Dollar, who still lived in Brockton, was going through all my recruitment letters for college. The first words out of his mouth grabbed my attention, "Yo, J.U. sent me a letter as well."

The next thing I knew, I was on the phone with Charlie Roman, defensive coordinator for Jacksonville University. He'd watched my highlight tapes and said that I would be great fit for the linebacker scheme he was implementing for the defense. He then offered me a partial scholarship and financial aid.

I called Don Dollar and asked, "Are you ready to go to Florida?!" He said, "Why not?" From that moment, we decided we were going to take over Florida together. There was no stopping us!

Don became my college roommate, which was very comforting and something I really needed in my life. It was good having a familiar face with me to start this new journey with.

My father's family resided in St. Augustine, which is only about 40 miles from Jacksonville. I figured being that close in proximity would give my dad more incentive to travel from Massachusetts to watch me play football at J.U. before he was able to move permanently. He could stay with his family to save money on hotels while searching for a new job.

In 1997, my freshman year was also the inaugural year for Jacksonville University's football team, the Dolphins. The team reported at school a month before the regular students. I knew I needed to adjust to the Florida heat before practice, so immediately after graduation, I moved to St. Augustine.

I will never forget that hot summer day when I set out for my first run to the Bridge of Lions. I ran 12 miles a day and was eager to achieve the best body possible when I reported to training camp in August. Before I arrived on campus, I'd already decided that my main goal was to make the traveling squad.

When August rolled around, the football team made up the only students on campus. This solitude allowed us to meet and get to know one another. In that first year, all our equipment was brand new—not a single scratch or scuff mark. It was great to have new equipment, but every piece needed to be broken in, including my helmet. Breaking in my helmet was a challenge with my little peanut head. Plus, I was always bald and didn't wear a headband, so my helmet constantly slid around.

A big shout out to the Jacksonville Jaguars, who donated their equipment to us to get us started. It was the inaugural year in 1997, as we were the first football team in the school's history.

Wearing official NFL equipment brought a surreal feeling with it. Eventually, we came to wear the real-deal equipment filmed on TV; the same equipment used in playoff games. Not only did we wear their official gear, we actually hung out with the players. Some sat on the sidelines and watched our practices. Occasionally, we went out to the clubs and ran into them in the city—life was good!

There was an older player on our team, Dre, who'd previously attended college but had forfeit his credits just to come in as a freshman and play football. Dre was like an uncle to us all; almost everything he said was law.

One evening, our team went out together to a local club. I had a fake ID and showed it to the door guy, who was standing right next to an undercover police officer.

The officer said very explicitly, "If you walk into this club, I'm going to arrest you." At this point, the team didn't know each other extremely well. A lot of the players still wanted to go in the club, despite this minor setback.

However, Dre said, "If Corey can't go in, then none of us go in." At that point, we all left with a stronger bond than ever. To this day, I still consider Dre my brother.

Since I was one of the few players on the team born outside Florida, I was hazed often because I didn't know the ways of the south. That was the great thing about the gridiron. The field was the great equalizer where the best man won. I knew I wasn't the best player on the field, but I knew I worked the hardest. While other players slept, I was in the gym.

My brother advised me that the best way to make the traveling squad was to play more than one position. "Making an impact on special teams is very important if you're trying to make it to the NFL," he said. I wasn't physically as big as the other players, but because my brother helped me hone my skills in high school as a long snapper, I could snap the ball extremely quickly and accurately. That gave me an edge and I held tightly to every advantage.

Every time I set foot on the field, the grass crunched under my cleats and I would breathe deeply, smelling the fresh cut turf. I took a moment to take it all in. It felt good; I knew I was meant to be here. I knew football would always be a great part of my life because I could not get enough of the sport. My desire to be the best at every drill, at every practice, and every position drove me to put forth more than one hundred percent effort at all times. I trusted that my will and work ethic would bring me to a place I wanted to be. As I mentioned earlier, I played my heart out with little regard to my body. At the time, schools did not have any concussion protocols. You could sustain a concussion and walk right back on the field without some type of medical intervention. Nothing stopped me though, not even the broken nose I suffered when I tackled another player. My helmet slid down the bar and broke my nose. Luckily, there wasn't any blood, but it hurt like a son of a bitch. I wasn't one to cave to pain and pushed through it in order to keep my cleats on the turf. It was all worth it in the end, when I found out I would become a starting linebacker.

There was a player on the Jaguars who I followed at the time, Natrone Means. He wore this Darth Vader-type visor, and I told myself I had to get one. I called up the equipment manager for the Jaguars, whom I'd met through our connections, and he sent one like it was nothing. That was power; I felt unstoppable. Wearing the visor felt like a coat of armor.

As much as I loved football, it did take up a lot of my time. I had to change my major from biology to communications since the biology labs were on Saturdays. Of course, Saturday lab time conflicted with our games. My love for football outranked my interest in biology. I found that studying, time management, and concentration were very difficult to maintain during my freshman year. Nevertheless, I had to maintain a 3.0 GPA. We had mandatory study hall and tutors who traveled with us to keep us on top of our academics.

I managed to find time for hanging out with friends. When offered the chance to drink alcohol, I didn't want anything to do with it—not after seeing what my mother went through. Both my father and my brother did not drink, and as they were both successful in their own right, I saw no reason to start drinking. I was afraid it would restrict my future. Alcohol just wasn't a part of my life, and I never felt like I was missing anything.

I spent a great deal of time with Dre and my boy from home, Don Dollar. We hung out with one of our coaches, Coach D, who had played in the NFL. He told us stories about playing at that esteemed next level and how great it was if you managed it properly.

The Valley Boys, who were the original football players, and Coach D and I, would go out to Jacksonville clubs downtown. I remember seeing players from the Jaguars, like Fred Taylor and Big Kev. And we would talk about the transition from college to the NFL. It was amazing seeing players we watched on TV within arm's reach. I felt confident that I'd be in their shoes one day. If I stayed on top of my classes and continued improving my football skills, I believed I would soon be driving fancy cars and my family would watch me play during Sunday NFL games on TV.

One of the hardest lessons I learned in my college years centered around a fraternity started at Howard University in 1911. When my brother came home for spring break, he told me that he saw many of the football players throwing up a unique hand symbol. I learned it was called "the hooks," which meant you were part of a predominately all-black order, known as the Omega Psi Phi Fraternity, Incorporated. I didn't know much about it, but I was curious. Coincidentally, the fraternity held an interest meeting at Jacksonville University and I desperately wanted to attend.

The night of the meeting, two men walked into the room who were members of the Omega Psi Phi Fraternity, Incorporated. The room got extremely quiet as they introduced themselves as Ghost and Lou of Chi Chapter located at Edward Waters College in Jacksonville. The meeting revolved around their order telling us they would not form a chapter at Jacksonville University and that if we were interested, we had to find them. The meeting piqued my interest even more, and I had to know everything about the fraternity.

So, later on that week, I went to seek them out. I drove out to Edward Waters College and found their frat house. The first brother I met was Slice, who I came to find out was the tail dawg on the 97 line. That means he was the last person to complete the line who was selected for the process of initiation. He asked, "Can I help you?"

I replied, "I want to be a part of your fraternity."

He busted out laughing because I had a thick Boston accent. He asked me if I was a cop. He didn't allow me to approach the frat house any further. He gave me instructions to come back tomorrow and he highly suggested for me to bring a box of Popeye's chicken and some drinks in order to meet the bruhs. The very next day, I borrowed a car and went back to E.W.C. with chicken in hand.

At first sight, I knew this was something I wanted to be involved in, but I had no idea what I was about to subject myself to. However, when I set my sights on something, I do not give up until I get it. I am one of the most determined people I know. I have an immense amount of passion that some people could call borderline crazy at times. When I'm focused on something, I will not let it go.

The pledge process was grueling, but I don't regret any of it. Some of my closest friends to this day are guys I met in that fraternity. Once again, alcohol reared its ugly head in my life. It was not part of the pledge to join the fraternity. Believe it or not, one of my coaches had suggested that I drink to pack on calories since I lost considerable weight during the pledging process and while still training and playing football.

In the fraternity environment, there was no escape from alcohol. I wanted to fit in with my line brothers better, so I heavily experimented with alcohol. I didn't like the taste of beer, but I couldn't afford mixed drinks, so I settled for beer. From the very beginning, I knew I had a problem.

My first sip of beer tasted bitter and dry. It didn't agree with me as well as I thought it would. I was in college now, a man, so I had to toughen up. I suppressed the taste of it and welcomed the buzz that followed. Enough buzzes created a bonding between my teammates and me. It wasn't my favorite way to sow my roots, but it was how everyone bonded. They all drank alcohol, so I felt at the time that I had to drink too.

When our team traveled for away games, the guys usually hung out the night before and drank. Sometimes, they stayed up the entire night. The solution was sleeping on the bus on the way to whatever city we were scheduled to play.

First, drinking was just for fun. Hanging out with the boys, going to parties, and dancing with the cute college girls. It all seemed harmless. But as the nights and weeks went on, I started drinking more heavily. It started to become an issue for me and affected my daily life. Other things in life didn't seem as important as going out drinking. It escalated to the point where I wasn't even going to parties anymore. I was just at home, drinking alone.

Sophomore year was mostly a blur, but I still managed to get on the field and play well. My junior year, I was still the starting linebacker, but not for long. The night before we left for Mississippi, I got extremely drunk alone and missed my alarm clock. I woke up after the team bus had already left, which I knew would land me in big trouble. I asked one of my teammates, Ricardo Tillman, for help. He refused to cover for me because he saw that my drinking was getting out of hand and told me I needed to get myself together. Hearing his bold advice became a pivotal point for me.

Ricardo ("Rico") was a beast on the field. He was one of the best wide receivers and team captains out of Miami-Dade County, Florida. He would always make fun of me because he thought I was awkward off the field. On the field, he wanted nothing to do with me. We both had love for football and a Miami-based rapper named Trick Daddy Dollars. One day, we were all in the dorms, and Rico was pissed because someone stole his *Based on a True Story* CD by Trick. I said, "Dawg, I have the CD." The room then got quiet and everyone looked at me. He busted out laughing and said, "Hell, nah! Where the hell did you get that CD?"

I replied, "B.C.R. (Black College Reunion) in Daytona Beach." And his mouth dropped. He said I was the whitest black person in all of Daytona for that reunion. The entire room erupted in laughter. Later that year, my dawg Rico, one of the original Valley Boys, was killed while helping one of the girls from my University at a night club. Rico was an amazing player, friend, captain, and man. (Rest in Paradise, King #8.)

I decided that playing football was no longer fun. Pledging took its place over football in terms of importance. I finished the season and never got my starting position back. With that, my dreams of getting to play for the NFL were gone. But honestly, I didn't even care. I was numb to it. I called my father and told him the whole story. He, of course, told my brother, who continually pushed my dad to bring me home to Massachusetts.

No matter what happened, I was not going back to Massachusetts.

After the season ended, I felt disconnected without football and hanging with my teammates. I saw no reason to stay in Jacksonville, but I still loved Florida. I wanted to transfer to the University of North Florida.

Since I wasn't playing football anymore, I had free time to get a job. I was going out clubbing a lot. Eventually, I found myself a job working as a security guard in one of the clubs.

At the same time as my decision to transfer, my father decided to move to Florida. Now, I finally had my father close by, a job, and my next step in my sights. Things were good and I thought my plans were solid. While I was in the process of making a transfer to the University of North Florida, I discovered that my financial aid was compromised. I didn't have the money to pay for my upcoming classes. I wasn't making enough money working part-time to pay for the tuition. This hit me really hard. How would I continue on with college? Mom and Dad didn't have enough money to float me. My depression started to set back in, and then there was another blow.

My father had a heart attack.

I couldn't focus on transferring at all now and spent all of my free time taking care of him. My drinking continued and turned excessive to where I reached my mother's level. Things were not looking good. I ended up dropping out of college because I couldn't afford the tuition. School provided structure and I needed to find something similar with discipline and new challenges. I realized that without structure, I go haywire. It's not good for my mental health.

Once my father's health improved, I could focus on myself again. I needed to plan out my next move. My father was a member of the special forces; therefore, joining the military seemed like the only logical answer.

CHAPTER 3
MILITARY LIFE

I once watched a movie about the Navy SEALs, starring Charlie Sheen. The specialized Sea-Air-and-Land unit was always in the back of my mind as I grew up. First, I loved the water. Every time I visited Florida as a kid, my cousins would send me out to steal crab traps. Boy, was it difficult, but I had perseverance and became a powerful swimmer in open water. Second, I strove to challenge myself with the biggest and baddest thing I could. So, I wasn't a complete stranger to the water.

I found the local recruiting office, but I kept it quiet from my father. The recruiter showed me a training video of SEALs involved in close-quarters combat (CQB) battles, an actual kill-house, night operations, and high altitude, low-opening (HALO) jumps. In HALO jumps, you deploy with a team out of a military platform at a high altitude (between 15,000 and 30,000 feet) and fall through the atmosphere, waiting until a low altitude to open your parachute. This unit was right up my alley since selection was extremely difficult—not everybody can become a SEAL. I enjoyed executing things that people said I could not. After the video, I told the recruiter that I wanted to sign up for the team.

As I filled out the paperwork, the recruiter informed me that there was a two-year waiting period. I couldn't simply sit around for two years and voiced my concerns by saying, "I just want to be involved somehow with the special forces." However, my other option, Special Warfare Combatant-Craft Crewman (SWCC) also brought a long waiting period. When I asked if I could do something just to get me into the fleet, he suggested becoming a rescue swimmer. In that moment, I was at my physical peak. I was muscular and strong from weightlifting and ready to go.

I was informed I'd be stationed in Great Lakes, Illinois, and that all of my training would occur in Florida. As soon as I arrived in Illinois, they saw I was both older and built. I was tasked with command of my regiment as part of the integrated division. The division was comprised of people with special skills, exceptional college backgrounds, or something else unique, like foreign languages.

My command provided us all with basic necessities for training. The boots that were issued were hard as hell on our feet, tough to break in, and we wore them every time we ran. I had to get up earlier than Reveille (Reveille is a standard military time to start the day) because I was given the opportunity to do Seal Physical Training (PT) before my command started their PT.

I was pulling double duty before 0500 and then I would come back to the barracks and mobilize the troops of my command and duties. We had to run up to three miles every other day, and as a result, huge blisters became an everyday occurrence. Our path was outside the camp and, when we ran through an intersection, crossing guards would stop traffic. One of my duties was to delegate the crossing guard duties, and in order to be equal, I needed two men and two women. However, the women in our group often suffered stress fractures from running. Those who didn't simply opted out. "Don't pick me today," they'd beg. The problem was, we didn't have anybody else to pick from.

On one particularly bad day, one girl became so upset, she went to the recruit division commander and complained, saying that I tried to sexually assault her. They brought me in and I was in shock. "When did this happen!? ...I don't understand what's going on!"

They repeated, "We know you did it."

What saved me was the training I endured with the SEALs. The commander in charge thought that these accusations against me didn't sound right. He sent me back to training—this time, to an all-male division. I was only two weeks away from graduating boot camp, but now I was placed back in week five. The woman eventually admitted she was just mad and that was her reasoning behind the accusation. But regardless, her words sent me to the back of the line. It really upset me because I don't like being accused of doing something when I'm innocent. Plus, having to endure more boot camp was not something I wanted to physically cope with. I don't like failures—they don't sit well with me. But I pushed through because that's what I do.

Finally, I graduated boot camp. My next stop was Naval Aircrew Candidate School (NACCS), the flight school in Pensacola, Florida, which lasted four weeks. Every day was the same. We woke up, we trained, and we ran. After lunch, we were obligated to four-hour pool workouts. My roommate at NACCS was a former running back from the University of Maryland. He and I competed with each other and built each other up. We always scored at the top of our class. He was on the Flight Engineer (FE) track and I was on the Aviation Warfare (AW). He always told me to score as high as possible because the top of the class gets to choose their orders around the world.

After graduation, I had no one telling me when and where to sleep. I actually had money. To celebrate, I started drinking again. On base, drinking was pretty much an accepted habit as long as you were of legal age. Everyone was drinking a lot every night and on the weekend. Once again, like in college, it was hard to get away from alcohol.

I was now in flight school, which was classified as "top secret." We could only bring in a pencil or a calculator; no loose papers could leave with us. I had never been in a plane like the P-3 Charlie that we used in training. Its original purpose was to track submarines. On a military plane, details are not for comfort; everything serves a specific function. The interior is bare bones, down to the metal frame. It's very "function-over-form." For example, if a circuit breaker short circuits, you need to easily access it for repairs. Any oil or hydraulic fluid leaks can quickly be found. There's no heater because the instruments run so hot. You sleep next to the instruments because they're giving off so much heat.

I planned on being a sensor two acoustic operator. An acoustic operator is a sound operator who drops sonar buoys to track enemy submarines. On a P-3, you have a sensor one, the senior acoustic operator; a sensor two, a non-senior qualified operator; and a non-acoustic sensor three, whose job is to check the weather and control the cameras and missiles. On board, we also had a pilot, co-pilot, and a flight engineer. We used it to assist the Drug Enforcement Administration (DEA), the U.S. Customs and Border Protection (CBP), and other federal law enforcement agencies. I was on track to becoming a qualified sensor two, but that was only a formality; we didn't do much of anything. There were no flights, no simulations, or live flights at this particular phase in my flight school. Basically, we performed the grunt work and learned the components of the position.

At the same time, we used graphs to measure the harmonics—sound vibrations given off by different vessels, different instruments, and different platforms. It was essential that we learned how to differentiate between instruments. We had to be proficient before we could explore the actual instruments on board. The fundamentals were essential in case our main systems broke down.

This flight school period lasted about a year. I became close with a guy named Rowe and another named Taylor. We referred to Rowe as "Black" because of how dark his skin was. Taylor pretty much lived in a shell. He was young and from Vallejo, California, one of the original homes of the hyphy movement. The word hyphy is Oakland slang meaning "hyperactive." More specifically, it's an adjective that describes the music and the urban culture associated with that area. Central to the hyphy movement was what Dre called "Thizz" or ecstasy. I took the two of them under my wing and became the wild one of the group. Since I was older and had a truck, we went on excursions together to places like New Orleans. We traveled and partied as much as age allowed. Rowe and Taylor were underage, and understandably, they didn't want to risk drinking, especially on base.

While we attended flight school, the most terrifying day in US history took place. Two airplanes were hijacked and flown into the World Trade Center.

Before 9/11, the military bases were considered somewhat laid back; you could gain access on or off base without any ID in most cases. Privileges like those disappeared on that fateful Tuesday.

I remember it like it was yesterday. We were in the middle of class. On the military base, everything is precise. Everything is in uniform, so you'd easily notice if something was off. We were taught to pay attention to the smallest details. That day, we watched our instructors' faces change into battle mode. Keep in mind that while we were in the classroom, people in our fleet were stationed in places like the Pentagon.

As we sat in the classroom getting nervous, the all-hands-on-deck alarm went off—a loud screeching siren followed by a stern voice, something I never even heard before. It said,

"General quarters, general quarters; this is not a drill."

As students, we wondered what the hell was happening. Our Command Master Chief informed us that the United States was under attack. All anyone could think was, *"What is this guy talking about?"* My heart dropped into my stomach. I got nauseated at the thought of what was going on outside the base. We were safe, but what about my family? Where was the attack taking place? Were they going to tell us what was going on?

We were inside this vault-like building that had a long passageway. The instructors had us line up against the wall, standing at attention. He said our base was on lockdown and all civilians had to be escorted out. If you saw a civilian, you must report them to the military police (MP). They kicked every civilian off Naval Air Station Pensacola within 30 minutes. By the time we left the classroom and returned to our barracks, no civilians remained on base. We looked up to see several F-18s circling overheard like vultures. Next came the tanks. I had no idea we even had tanks on our naval base!

Everybody was restricted to the base perimeter. If you were off base, you could not come back on base. If you were on base, you could not leave. Civilians were the ones who usually worked in the galleys, so we now had to serve our own food. In just minutes, we went from a relaxed base to 50 planes and tanks operating in defense. Protocol dictated that large cement dividers were set up, so everyone had to move carefully in vehicles. No one could make a phone call because the phone lines were dead. The only exception was military phones.

The F-18s circled the base all night and class was canceled. I recall they even restricted alcohol. There was no drinking allowed and they closed the bars. Everything that happened was straight out of a movie; I never saw anything like it. From then on, there were very strict rules. You could no longer have visitors meet you on base. The strict orders remained like that all the way until I graduated.

When I did graduate from A school, I received a $15,000 bonus and was off to my next school, which was Survival Evasion Resistance and Escape Training (S.E.R.E.) located in Brunswick, Maine. S.E.R.E. was 1,000% real. We would hear things about how officers peed themselves and how others even died. S.E.R.E was designed to teach you how to properly keep your mouth shut if you were caught behind enemy lines, to endure unimaginable torture, and to give the proper information in accordance with the Geneva Convention. Because of my past journeys embarked upon in college, I looked forward to this phase of training. When I reported to Brunswick, Maine, I saw some friendly faces, Rowe and Taylor. I couldn't stop laughing because my boy Taylor was so scared, he acquired the ability to stutter overnight. I told him, "Don't worry, the worst case scenario is that you'll die."

Due to my military obligation, I can't go into further details about S.E.R.E, but I can say it's a necessary evil and I appreciate the men and women who are afraid, but go anyway. To the agents and instructors responsible for my training, thank you.

After we graduated S.E.R.E., we moved on to our fleet replacement training in Jacksonville at VP-30, which was a training squadron. I found myself back in the city where I'd attended college, the same city where I'd pledged to join the fraternity—where my adult life all began. Outside of my drinking, I had a pocket full of money and I was doing well in life.

The first part of fleet replacement training was our computer-based trainings, which we needed to pass before executing live flights. I felt so comfortable there, I called it my second home. My brothers from the fraternity were part of the training and they were like my family. I had almost zero responsibility. I did cook a lot, which I found to be enjoyable. I had all the money I needed, I didn't have to pay rent, and I had access to everything I wanted. I could eat, drink and party. However, I had literally no direction—something I found to be a necessity for my own personal success.

Without solid direction, I did still graduate from fleet replacement training and with flying colors. My father attended my graduation, which was a tremendous rush, given his military background and love for me.

In retrospect, I thought the military would give me what I searched for, but it only fueled my pain and misery.

I FOUND ME

CHAPTER 4
STRUGGLES IN THE MILITARY

After graduation of the first part of flight training, which was basic knowledge of the aircraft, we could grab flights on the weekends to destinations like Spain, San Diego, and Hawaii. They called it a NAV Extended, a "training exercise." In fact, the military had to burn the fuel; basically use it or lose it, so it worked out for us. It was a great perk after all of our hard work. However, it took our partying to a whole 'nother level.

I still had to do computer classes at the base, but I wasn't taking the computer-based trainings seriously. The instructor asked why I continually failed the tests. I didn't realize they counted for so much of our grade, so I breezed through them. They ended up putting me into a mandatory study hall until my test scores improved. I of course didn't want to go; I wanted to see my friends instead.

So, one night, I left base to hang out at Ghost's house. Ghost was from the fraternity and lived on the north side of Duuuuval. Ghost is like a father figure to me. Even back in the day when I was on the line pledging in college. It wasn't a nice area, but that didn't bother me much. But it probably wasn't the best place for me to be. I should have been studying for my classes, but my demons got the best of me instead.

All night, I drank and we reminisced together about the old days. Around 3:00 a.m., I told him I needed to leave because I had class in the morning. I got into my car and headed home. The next thing I remembered, everything went black. The only thing I could remember was Ghost saying, "I love you; get home safe."

I vaguely remember hearing cars, people talking, and plenty of sirens off in the distance. My head was pounding something fierce. I was on the side of the road. I was no longer in my truck. Where was my truck?!

I had been carjacked.

While I was sitting at a light with my window down, I'd been struck with a crowbar. I never even saw it coming. They hit me good on the head, pulled me out, and left me on the side of the road for dead. I don't even know how long I was out. Someone must have seen it happen and called 911.

When the paramedics arrived, they sent me back to the base instead of the hospital. I had to stand before the Command Master Chief with dried blood on my face and my head throbbing like it was going to explode. He kept asking if the incident was drug-related. Naturally, he wanted to know why I was in that rough neighborhood at that time of night. I explained I was from the area and knew people who lived there. I'd modified my truck when I received my military bonus after graduation, which I assumed had made me a target.

My Military Chief heard my story and added his two cents. "You are messing up beyond measure. You're like a zebra, because you can't change your stripes." Chief and I would spend hours talking about life and the fleet since the first day I checked in BP-30 at NAS Jax. I had so much respect for this man, I was at a loss for words and felt great shame. He told me to go to medical and they did a full-flight medical workup and removed me from flight status because of my injuries. After I was released from medical, Chief called me and told me to meet him at his house. When I arrived, he gave me $200 and told me he believed in and loved me. He said, "Hall, are you going to be a zebra that changes your stripes or just exist and take up oxygen?" I couldn't move; my mind was running and I couldn't stop it. Chief looked me in the eye one more time and simply walked back to his house.

About an hour later, command told me the guy who stole my truck was arrested in a small town called Soperton, Georgia. When they found him, they called me to come get my vehicle. I'd suffered a concussion and couldn't see or walk well, but I still had to go get my truck. Luckily, I was able to get Rowe and Taylor to drive me to Georgia. When we arrived, I had to fork over $400 in towing fees. I didn't have the money at the time, so I had to call my father.

My poor father didn't know what happened to me. The police had called him and said I was basically left for dead on the side of the road somewhere in Jacksonville. He was freaking out when I called. His mixed emotions came out in full force—crying in sadness and then joy and pure, sharp anger directed toward my carjacker. He had to wire the money via Western Union, but they didn't open until the following morning. The fellas and I sat in the field and told jokes until morning. Once it was morning, we went to Western Union. In line, the man in front of me had a brand I recognized. We spoke and he asked a series of questions. Come to find out, his cousin from Tuskegee had pledged at Lambda Epsilon. He was actually one of the brothers that I knew well when I was on line in college. He asked me what was his cousin famous for? I answered and a smirk rose on his face. He then asked if I had eaten, and if I needed any money. If I needed anything at all, all I had to was ask and he had my back. I said no thank you, and he demanded that I take $20 and have his cousin call him when I got back to Jacksonville. Rowe and Taylor said that fraternity stuff is deep. Roe asked me, "How in the hell do you remember all that shit he asked you, but you don't know where you live?" They all started laughing. I said, "You have to pledge in order to understand."

After returning with my truck, I was taken out of training to recover from the carjacking. While I recovered from the actual concussion, I still felt off. I wasn't really sure what it was. But things were different. Something happened when that crowbar hit me.

When I was ready to go back to base, I decided I was not going alone. After being carjacked, I wanted to carry my sidearm that I'd been keeping at my father's house. I didn't even consider the amount of trouble a gun could bring me. I was solely focused on my own safety at that point.

Post recovery, I was sent back to training. I was in charge of reading the pings, which was what a sonar buoy would send back to the plane in order to locate, find the range, and set the depth and speed of our target. The best of the best could gauge the country, based on the cavitation, or sound readings you received from the propellers. I loved the process and my duty. We had PT at 0600 hours (6:00 a.m. for non-military personnel), which lasted 45 minutes, then returned to the barracks. We showered and had breakfast brought to us.

I had to know each sonar buoy—they used to call them "Cadillacs" because one sonar buoy cost as much as an Escalade. We dropped roughly 60 buoys during the process of tracking a submarine.

In the military, you're supposed to arrive 15 minutes early for all your duties. If you are not 15 minutes early, you're late. One day, I showed up 12 minutes early to class, which meant I was three minutes late.

Base personnel came to my class and told me to get my dress whites, and said I had to go see the skipper. I didn't understand why because class hadn't started. I knew I'd needed to be there 15 minutes before, but for some reason the 12 and 15 just didn't click in my brain. It was like I didn't really care. It's only a three-minute difference. What's the big deal? Well, it was a BIG deal.

I had to stand in a hallway for six hours straight. I couldn't move. I couldn't use the restroom. I couldn't eat. Six hours later, two guards escorted me to another room. My Chief was present in the room, but he didn't speak a word. I couldn't believe that it was this serious. I was a petty officer at this point. The commanding officer asked me, "Do you think your actions are in accordance of a petty officer third class in the US Navy?"

I responded, "Yes."

He yelled, "No!"

He then added, "Petty Officer Hall, I will suspend penalty if this doesn't make any sense to you."

I said, "Okay."

He yelled, "This is not a question!"

The commanding officer stated that I was accused of unauthorized absence, which was a violation of the article 86 of the Uniform Code of Military Justice (UCMJ) as I was three minutes late to flight training. Here is your scenario: now you are on a tactical mission and your missiles are three minutes off target. How many innocent people did you kill? Even worse, you could be on a classified mission in a country we did not have permission to be in. For your three minutes, we now have an international incident that cost lives, money, careers, and sleep.

Right then and there, I was stripped of my rank. I dropped two ranks in a matter of minutes. With that terrifying explanation, I understood the gravity of the situation. I lost two months' pay in one day and was sentenced to ten days in the brig for every minute I was late. As a result, I spent 30 days in the brig for being three minutes late to class. He then stated, "Airman Hall you are amazing at your job, which is why Chief suggested that we start you in training from where you left off. You have a lot to offer, make it count after your sentence is complete."

During those long 30 days, I had inspection every day. The guards woke us up on the hour for us to make our beds and stand for inspection. Then, after the inspection, we could go back to sleep. Their intention was to re-instill everything that we learned in boot camp. It was called "corrective custody." We did minuscule, tedious work from sun up to sun down.

For example, after we stripped and buffed the floor, they made us strip it and buff it again. That was the cleanest facility known to mankind. In case you're wondering, if someone already in the brig got in trouble, they were put on restriction, with only bread and water, similar to going into solitary confinement. I was not trying to push my luck. I understood that my mistake had cost a lot, especially the large amounts of money used to correct a mistake that could have been avoided in the first place. I was probably harder on myself than their punishment could have ever been. I couldn't believe I let myself slip up, so I busted my ass during that time to try to make up for it.

I was released from the brig two days early for good behavior. Amazingly, I was late my first day out. The good thing was that no one knew I was out of the brig yet because I wasn't supposed to be released for two more days. I ended up skipping the inspection that we had. I thought I got away with it, but two weeks later, they caught on and the whole place erupted. They realized everything I got away with and placed an open-book Naval Air Training Operations Procedures and Standardization (N.A.T.O.P.S.) test in front of me. They said, "Hall, everyone here loves you, but we can't do it for you. This test will dictate what happens next. You pass, you go to Hawaii like you want and move on in accordance with your orders. You fail, and we strip you of everything and send you to the fleet in Norfolk, Virginia, undesignated."

I had to take the exam, which I failed. I had dream orders to end up in Hawaii, and they took those dreams away. They changed my orders to Virginia. This was another blow to my ego. Things were starting to slip away from me.

For some reason, I knew I should not being doing the things I was doing, but it was like I couldn't control my own actions. Something inside of me was taking over. I felt that my rational mind was floating outside of me, knowing right from wrong, and I was a bystander watching it all slowly derail. I didn't want to be late or skip out on stuff, but I was like a puppet as there were strings I did not control.

With Hawaii dreams washed away in a tsunami of my own destruction, I had time to kill before my Virginia orders, so I returned to my father's place. I needed some extra money since my pay was cut in half due to my loss in rank. So, I did security at a few of the local night clubs in my dad's city of Melbourne, Florida. A coworker said he was in need of a firearm. I couldn't bring mine to Virginia with me, so I planned to sell my gun to him.

This guy lived in a nice neighborhood in Melbourne. I went over to his house one night to sell him the pistol and we ended up hanging out for a while. He started pouring drinks and before we knew it, we were wasted. Not the best combination—money, alcohol, and a firearm. In his intoxicated state of mind, he started to question the capabilities of the gun. He got paranoid and thought I was going to sell him one that didn't work. Of course that wasn't the case I argued. So, to illustrate my point, I fired the gun and hit a jacuzzi this guy had in his living room. He was so drunk, he didn't even care, so I just kept shooting. He was more happy that it was a functioning weapon! I wish I was making this up.

Happy with his new purchase, but I hadn't given him the gun yet, we moved our party to an after-hours club. We partied for a while and then met some friends with the intention of bringing them back to his jacuzzi, which I forgot had fresh bullet holes. But that didn't put a damper on our intentions. As we drove back listening to the Trick Daddy that I loved, I pulled into his cul-de-sac.

I was so drunk that for a moment, I thought all the houses had flashing Christmas lights on. Then I realized it was cop cars. Policemen were standing at every door. I tried to turn around, but it was too late; I noticed a helicopter flying above us. I looked in my rearview mirror and saw a fleet of squad cars. That morning, I got arrested for the first time, because I still had the gun on me.

I FOUND ME

This was a point in my life where alarms should have been going off. I had never heard of the term "bipolar," but later I found out the military should have tested me for it. I did not know at the time I had bipolar disorder. No one else knew, either. All I knew was that it seemed like my life was spinning out of control. Everything that I worked so hard for, I kept destroying.

I got released from jail and the police sent me back to the military. I was labeled a black sheep. Everyone knew what had happened, since gossip spreads like wildfire there. I wrongfully earned the nickname "Shooter."

I was placed in a unit of outcasts, and we each had to wear a black arm band like a scarlet letter. I still awaited my orders to Virginia. Some of the guys informed me they were headed on a road trip to Miami. I thought that sounded like a good way to burn some time, so I decided to tag along.

We arrived at the hotel in Miami, where I got my own room. It got real pretty quickly. Again, I found myself in a black hole of alcohol. Some of the cats I was with came in and said they had hit a lick (robbery). Reality hit me like a fucking train. My thoughts were that the room was in my name and if anyone got hurt. This couldn't be happening. I sat there frozen, wondering how I let myself get into these terrible situations. I hadn't even settled into my room yet or unpacked my suitcase. How the hell did they already commit a crime?! I waited for one of two groups of people, either hitmen to kill us or the police to arrest us.

I never dealt with the reality of situations well. My solution was to drink problems away. In my drunken stupor a few hours later, there was a knock on the door. "Room service!" said a disguised voice. I didn't order any room service, and before I could answer, the Miami SWAT team busted in through the door. They put me under arrest and took me in for questioning. Eventually, I was locked up.

Sometime later, for unknown reasons, the judge let me go. I called the base and reported where I had been. They told me I was to report to Jacksonville by the next morning, but my truck had been impounded and they wouldn't release it back to me. So far, it was the lowest point in my life.

So many bad decisions and so much bad luck came my way. I just didn't want to be in my body anymore; I couldn't deal with it. I felt like I was completely out of control. I knew I shouldn't be doing these things or placing myself in these bad situations, but I couldn't regulate it.

That night in Miami, I attempted suicide. I swallowed a handful of pills and washed them down with a 12-pack of beer. When nothing immediate happened, I decided I might as well try to make my way to Jacksonville. Whatever happened, happened. I took a bus to Jacksonville; by the time I arrived, I was extremely sick. I remember vomiting a nasty black mixture. I returned to my barracks, where I thought I was going to die. I just wanted it all to be over.

I made a call to my family members I made in college, Ghost and Lou. They said, "Dawg, we need to put some heat to your ass and get you back on track."

They gave me the number to an amazing attorney named Big Bruh.

At this time in my life, I was tired of feeling pain and causing pain. I was afraid and didn't know how to ask for help. To anyone feeling this way or who knows anyone in a black hole such as this, ask for help. I was told that I couldn't make a change if I couldn't make it to the next morning.

CHAPTER 5
PRISON AND COCAINE

I somehow managed not to die from the lethal mixture I took that night. Thankfully, the attorney I contacted, Big Bruh, helped me get out of all the trouble I was in. His legal footwork put me on mailing probation, meaning I didn't to have check in or perform any drug tests. I simply mailed in my forms saying that I accepted a job and provided an address. That was the first step in moving forward.

My attorney said, "I'll help you this one time, because I know you don't have the money to afford my services. And because you need to clear your name. You need to get your life together and I can't help you the next time you get into trouble. You're going to cook me crabs and surrender all of your weapons to me."

I replied, "Even my AK?" He looked at me like I was just as crazy as when I was on line pledging.

I told myself I would never get in trouble again.

It was finally time to report to Virginia, the last place I wanted to go after I'd been stripped of my ranks. I was treated like a grunt who'd just exited boot camp. I didn't appreciate that, especially after putting three years into the military, so I left.

I went absent without official leave (AWOL) and returned to Florida to see the one woman in my life. When I was around her, it made everything seem better, if only for a little while. I was restless in Virginia. I didn't want to be there, so I made the reckless decision to just up and leave without telling anyone.

I met my girlfriend during college one night when we were all at the club. My line brothers and I went out to our favorite hotspot and she and her friend came over to us. They both had British accents; I thought she was beautiful. We kept in contact and she often hung out with my friends and I. She knew my history, she knew my friends, and she loved me. Her job took her to Tampa, but she still met up with me when she could. When I sneaked down to see her, we spent some time in a hotel on the beach. Then, before I knew it, I had to travel back to Virginia. Memories like those kept me going when times got tough.

I was still under contract with the military, but I kept leaving because I was so detached from everything. Then I met a guy named Robbie, who was also in the air crew and underwent the same training I did. However, he lived as a civilian because he was excused for asthma. He was the head of security for a place called the Beach House in Virginia Beach. I got so tight with Robbie, he let me stay with him. I told him I would pay for rent by cooking for him.

I started cooking again while stationed in Virginia because food for me was like therapy. I really enjoyed coming up with recipes and being creative with different types of food. I was also really good at it; just a natural, I guess. Cooking helped me deal with my anxiety.

Since I didn't have much money, I helped myself to the frozen storage designated for the officers' mess hall. The freezers went down on the USS Washington and they put me on a 1,000-man working party. I noticed nobody checked hazmat going off the ship, so I grabbed a box of hazmat bags and went shopping on the flight deck where subzero storage was kept.

Staying with Robbie and cooking for him and everyone else who worked at the Beach House was the perfect getaway.

One day after my duties, I went out drinking with a shipmate. But this time I thought I was smart. I had him drive my truck because I was intoxicated. He suggested we go to a strip club and get some wings. We arrived at a random strip club in Virginia Beach. I looked around and commented, "I thought you said we were going to a strip club?"

He replied, "This is a strip club. It's called GoGo's."

I exclaimed, "Homie, if you want to go to a strip club, go to the bottom (Miami) and hit Rolex or King of Diamonds (KOD)." I was hungry, so I ordered wings and I brought them with me to eat while we were driving home. We climbed into my big fancy truck. I had it all decked out. You could see us coming a mile away. Nice rims, brightly colored paint, really dark tinted windows—it was sick.

Almost immediately after pulling out of the parking lot, we got pulled over. The officer asked me for my ID. He said I was intoxicated, to which I replied, "But I'm not driving." The driver was the one who was drunk. But, again, the problem was my flashy truck.

The officer said, "If you don't step out of the truck, I'm going to break your window."

I replied, "I promise you don't want to do that." Then the cop opened my door and tried to be rough with me. He said, "Now you're going to jail." When he grabbed me, I just reacted. My training took over and I locked him up and slammed him onto the hood of my truck. The other cop had a look of shock on his face. I walked over to him, turned around, and said, "I will let you arrest me." He didn't say a word and just cuffed me. The other cop got up and started talking shit while I was cuffed. I wanted to say he was telling the other officer to remove the cuffs, but at this point, I was so numb and defeated I couldn't make out the exact conversation between them.

I was arrested for public intoxication as a passenger in a car. Man, was I pissed! If you looked up the definition of furious, you'd find a picture of my face. As I sat in the back of the cop car, I wondered if they were going to eat my chicken wings.

Approximately six hours later, I was released to the custody of the Navy and was told to get my ass back to base by the officer on duty at the jail. But I didn't follow his orders. Instead, I went to the Beach House, where everyone was drinking at work—not a smart move. I climbed behind the wheel of my truck to go home and crashed it, getting hit with my first DUI. As a result, the team at work passed around a tip jar to collect my bail money. With enough time and tips, I made bail and returned to the Beach House. They told me that we all make mistakes and that I was family. Plus, they loved to watch me fight at the end of the night at closing. I was thankful they'd all pitched in and helped me out.

My life got to the point where everyone knew I was coming to the beach to fight. I hated Virginia so much, I was always talking shit about it. I was running my mouth, being loud and obnoxious in public. But I didn't care. I did not want to be there anymore.

One day after being released again, I called one of my boys who stayed off base. Because of the shame, I did not want to return back to the USS *George Washington*. He said I could lay low at his house because he and his girlfriend were visiting family in another state. I told him I didn't have a key, but he said to just go through the window like before, because a family member had his spare key. So, I went in through the window.

Later that evening, I tried to get a ride to the beach because my truck was totaled. A group of guys in the hood said they would drive me down to Virginia Beach. I got in their car and, before I knew it, they were taking me somewhere else. When I realized it, we got into a fight. One of the guys had a gun and his friends told him to shoot me. I managed to grab the gun and said, "If you don't let me out, I'll kill everyone."

They obeyed and I stepped out. I walked back to my boy's apartment because I felt that the night was already getting away from me, so I climbed back through the window and went to bed.

The next morning, Norfolk PD woke me up. I said, "May I help you?" They said there was a report of a burglary. I replied, "Not here; I've been here all night." The police asked me if I was supposed to be there. I answered yes and told them to call my friend. They did, and he told them I was allowed to be there. However, his girlfriend informed them that the place was in her name and she said she disagreed. So, I got arrested—again.

All these arrests violated my probation from the jacuzzi incident in Melbourne. I reported back to base and updated my command authority on what happened. I saw this as an excuse to get back to Florida, and honestly, I didn't wait to hear what they had to say. I jumped on the next flight to Jacksonville and planned to lay low with Ghost and Lou. I made a call to my brother from another (Dre). He said, "Boy, where you at?"

I replied, "Jax."

He replied, "I'm on my way." We partied another night in Jacksonville and then I went back to Tampa with Dre and the fellas that came to get me.

By this time, my baby took a job that would take her from England to Tampa. Since I was basically a fugitive, I didn't want to bring the heat to her door. She talked me into turning myself in again.

This was a really depressing time in my life. I felt like I was spinning out of control again. Everything I did just made it worse. I was getting sucked into a black hole and I honestly didn't know how to stop it. I knew I needed to get my life back in order, so I eventually turned myself in. I decided I needed to face the music.

I ended up doing approximately five months in jail because of the continuances. My head was in a really bad place at the time; nothing was adding up.

My girlfriend and I dated the entire time I was in the military. We met while we were both in college. Back when I still had my Hawaii orders, I asked her to marry me. She said she couldn't because Hawaii was "like an eleven-hour time difference." While I was in federal custody, her company was acquired by another establishment. That merger translated to her work visa being nullified. I had to find a way to marry her so she could stay.

I did my time. The judge said I was free, so naturally, I thought I was free. They just reinstated my original probation, which would conclude in one month's time. Upon completion of my probation, my record would be wiped clean. Then I was told Naval Criminal Investigative Services (NCIS), or the Feds, had a hold on me.

As it turned out, I had no documentation showing I had permission to be in Florida, so they assumed I'd deserted my position. So, I was then in custody for another week after being released from the judge.

One week later, two men from NCIS came to extradite me. They had two tickets for me, one to Fort Leavenworth, Kansas, and the other to Norfolk, Virginia. I told them I didn't know anyone in Kansas.

They replied, "When you want to shoot at people on the streets, still in the military, you go to Leavenworth."

I replied, "You have the wrong person."

He asked me for my last four of my social and my name. I answered and he said, "Yup, that's you." I was whisked away to the Orlando International Airport and placed shackled in the back of the plane to face desertion charges in Virginia.

When I had my day in court, I was allowed to present my case and was acquitted because my paperwork that I had accumulated added up. After that judge ordered my immediate release back to my command, which was the USS *George Washington*, I was arrested again. At this point, I was screaming "Double Jeopardy" to the heavens. The master-at-arms told me to shut up. He said new commend, new charges.

While awaiting my final court martial, I had been in custody approximately 70 days on board the USS *George Washington* docked in Virginia. While I was in custody, I was communicating with my girlfriend back in Tampa. She told me that her company was bought out and her new company wasn't going to reissue work visas. So, the only way for her to stay in America was to get married. I got one of the guards to sneak me out of brig so I could marry her at the courthouse. To this day, I still can't believe he agreed. Right after we left the courthouse, my wife hopped on a flight back to Tampa and I went right back to the brig. We had our official ceremony after I was released, but I can always say I loved her enough to risk my freedom to marry her.

After my final court martial, the captain suspended any further jail time and granted me a discharge from the United States Navy, avoiding a dishonorable discharge. While filling out my final paperwork for discharge, the admin asked me when I got married. I just pointed to the date because the whole time, they'd stopped my pay. So, they had to backdate it to when I'd gotten married. I was extremely sick at the time, but I wasn't a dummy. For the first time in a long time, I felt alive.

I went to one last party in Virginia after my hearing, where I was first introduced to that famous white girl—cocaine. I was drinking at a party, but I had not been in the presence of cocaine before, so I decided to try it. I instantly liked it. The feeling was euphoric! How had I never had this before? It made me feel like Superman. I was unstoppable. I had so much energy. With each line, my brain started to change.

The next morning, I was supposed to catch a train to Florida. I was still buzzing from all the white powder and booze. I was on the train and completely forgot to grab my connecting train because I was so stuck inside my manic thoughts. Next thing I knew, I was in Washington, D.C.

CHAPTER 6
LIFE AFTER THE MILITARY

After I was released from the military, I traveled to Tampa to be with my wife. I thought things would be different once I arrived. I didn't want to drink, but I just couldn't stop. I was addicted; I had no other way to cope with the stress in my life.

My wife suggested I go see a doctor. I didn't really see the point, assuming he or she would just tell me I was an alcoholic—a conclusion I'd already arrived at on my own.

However, she was getting fed up with my behavior. Once again, I felt like I was out of control. My shifts in mood were all over the place. Up, down, left, right; I never knew which direction I was going.

Eventually, I took my wife's advice and spoke with a doctor. Long story short, I was diagnosed as bipolar, with depression and insomnia. The sad fact I was told was that with three diagnosed conditions, figuring out which medications would treat me was a game of trial and error.

With my new diagnoses and the medications I was prescribed, I felt like I was starting to get myself back into order. At least now I had an answer as to why I was doing the things I did. I believe you first need to understand the why and that helps us take back control over ourselves. It all started to make sense now. I wasn't crazy, I had an illness.

So, I went back out on the job hunt and I landed one at a strip club in Tampa as security, thanks to my former experience. I was still into fighting, so that move seemed like a good fit. I was able to be aggressive, I got to fight sometimes, but I still received discipline like from within the military. It wasn't a normal nine-to-five job and it felt good to be working again.

The bad thing was that the appearance of the famous white lady was everywhere—cocaine was everywhere in that industry. The girls did it, the patrons wanted it, and the employees supplied it.

I managed to stay clean for a while by keeping to myself, but eventually, the temptation was too much. We had late night shifts, and everyone got off around 3 a.m. and would go out and party.

The undercover dealers in the joint had a large operation in motion. Every Wednesday, about a kilo and half were delivered, which lasted everyone through the weekend. I didn't have to pay for any drugs, and ended up doing more than I should have. I was also taking my medications to appease my wife, but they only slowed me down as they were suppressants. To counteract the feeling, I used cocaine to wind me back up. It took all my pain away, and I was using on a daily basis.

My wife didn't understand the full extent of my issues at the beginning. It got out of control so fast—it was constantly escalating. I only saw how cocaine brought me out of my misery, not how it compounded my problems, and the issues snowballed quickly.

She noticed that my behavior was changing and knew something was up, so I told her about my use. She didn't know how to handle the news. She'd never known anyone who used cocaine; it was foreign to her. I just knew that it made me feel better. I was self-medicating.

My wife and I then decided that we should travel to Los Angeles to visit my family. She thought that going there would help me with my issues. My mother was staying out there with my brother, who was acting in a hit show on BET called *The Game*.

My mother was still drinking, but I especially wanted to see her. I thought I could better relate to her problem now that we shared the same alcohol dependency. My wife and I spent a total of two weeks out there. During the first week, I severed my Achilles tendon in a pick-up basketball game. My bipolar medications caused me to gain weight and I wasn't as quick on my feet as I used to be. I was going for a lay-up and my tendon simply snapped.

My brother rushed me to the hospital, but when I got there, the doctor said it was just a sprain. They sent me home without doing anything for it. The rest of my time in L.A., it hurt really bad and I couldn't even walk on it. I knew something was definitely wrong.

When I returned to Florida, I saw an orthopedic surgeon. He said I needed to be in surgery right away. Unfortunately, my tendon already started to heal by attaching itself to a lower calf muscle. There was nothing connected to my foot! The surgeon needed to use a fiber mesh replacement, since, due to the scar tissue, they couldn't pull my Achilles tendon back down to my heel. The surgery was successful, so I could retain the use of my foot. The hospital staff gave me a bunch of Vicodin for the pain, but I didn't like the way they made me feel. Instead, I used my own pain killers—alcohol and cocaine.

My wife's job sometimes required her to travel for several weeks at a time. On one hand, I looked forward to her leaving, so I could party, but I also hated to see her leave. I felt lost and abandoned, just as I was when my father and brother left me when I was younger. My wife tried everything she could to help me. We finally came to the conclusion that I should enter a rehabilitation program. I made it through every step of the program, but I relapsed immediately after finishing. I considered it a double relapse because I went back to drinking *and* cocaine.

My wife really struggled with being the only source of income for the two of us. My student loans were deferred to the max, and I couldn't push them off any longer. I was in a really bad place. I felt scared to leave the house during the day, yet I managed to sneak out for cocaine. I spent most of my time sleeping.

My therapist suggested I apply for disability based on my mental health issues. I went through SSI to apply for disability, which took forever. One positive outcome from all of this stress was that my student loans would be written off because I was medically incapable of working. Overnight, approximately $64,000 was wiped off of my conscience.

When I received my disability application, I was denied. To fight the denial, I hired an attorney and re-applied. Again, I was denied and another year of my life passed. I was told, based on my medical records and my appearance at the hearing, that there was a job somewhere in the world that I could perform. They were telling me I was definitely less than one hundred percent disabled and capable of working. My next step was to file an appeal.

After dealing with two denied applications for disability income, I found the Master Masons. I thought they would be the solution to all of my problems via their stability and brotherhood. These were two reoccurring factors in my life that I always sought out one way or another. I need structure to keep myself in line. However, I always looked outside of myself for that discipline. What I really needed to do was look inside. So, attending that organization didn't work because I, again, didn't apply myself to the level I should have. I did become a Master Mason in 2008 and reached my ninth degree.

I went off on another bender and owned another firearm at the time. I just wanted to blow my own head off. I was so coked out of my mind that I wanted to stop the pain for everyone else. I thought I needed to kill myself to solve everyone else's problems. I went to rehab again, this time to a program in Bradenton, FL. I received a call that my cousin, whom I used to party with, hung himself. I went to his funeral and thought, *"This is where I'm heading. This will be me."* It was a scary moment for me. Going to his funeral shook me to my core. When I looked into the casket, all I saw was my own corpse lying there, stiff, and I knew I had to change.

After the funeral and second rehab program, I was improving. My father was still in Melbourne on the eastern Florida coast, and I was living in Tampa. He often called me to help him get members of our family together. I drove up to North Carolina, picked up my uncle, who was going through similar issues to me, and headed back to my father's place. I made that round trip four different times. Driving from Tampa to North Carolina to Melbourne to North Carolina to Tampa counted as one trip. I did it all because my father was elderly, and my uncle was in so much pain and misery. So, I did whatever I could to enjoy a happy moment with my family.

Then I got a call that my uncle had shot himself. In a short amount of time, I lost my uncle, my cousin who had committed suicide, and then my mom passed. I realized there was a pattern emerging. My family had a mental illness. I did not want to end up like them. I did not want their tragedy to be my legacy.

I watched a lot of Anthony Bourdain and Andrew Zimmern's cooking shows. I really admired them and their talents.

In her downtime, my wife applied for kitchen and cooking jobs for me. She knew that cooking was what brought me peace and great joy.

My wife was at her wit's end. I tried to do my best, but it wasn't enough. I believed there was a hidden solution, but I couldn't figure out what it was. When she told me I'd gotten an interview, she was more thrilled than I was. I didn't want to interview, but I felt like I had to go to make an effort. Emotionally, I was so detached from the entire job process. But when I went to the interview and was asked about my skills, I immediately became interested. It seemed like something I would enjoy doing.

I got the job, which was fantastic. It kept me on track for a while, but the restaurant industry also has a high rate of drug use. So, once again, I was in an environment where it was the norm for people to abuse drugs and to drink on the job. Almost everyone working in a kitchen was on cocaine to perform at their peak.

Then one day, she said she had to go to Penang, Malaysia, for work. Not long after, I noticed I had a mountain of cocaine on the table in the living room and I was alone and feeling defeated again and couldn't understand why.

I made the decision that I wanted it all to stop. So, I made a call to my Valley Boys from college, Josh and Dre, to come over. I didn't know what to do. I lost my mind. When they arrived, Josh called EMS and Dre flushed everything and said, "We love you."

I can remember this tragic moment as we started talking about a time back in college where we stole a two-man canoe to go fishing at 3 a.m. and got stuck in the middle of St. Johns River.

EMS arrived and stated that I was having a manic episode, so I got Baker Acted.

My doctor changed my medication and prescribed me lithium to slow me down. It worked, but it wasn't a be-all and end-all solution. By taking lithium, I would be great for part of the day, then the medication wore off and put me into a depression. It was like nothing in any aspect of my life was being properly managed. My doctor said I needed to spend a week at the facility in Bradenton again, making it my third attempt at rehabilitation. I was asking for help, but when I got the help, I fought it. That's the contradiction of bipolar disorder.

In the midst of all of this, my wife and I had been trying to have a baby for a while. It had been a long time since I last used or drank; everything regarding my health was improving. My wife got pregnant, which was great news.

Then the doctors said they didn't do treatment for *both* substance abuse and mental instability, so they just sent me home. I was kicked out without any solution or major improvements. It seemed as though nobody could help me.

So, I eventually found a new place for treatment, which provided me a scholarship for a 30-day treatment program. The whole time, I was afraid of being away from home for so long.

For 30 days, I applied myself and got back into the gym. Exercising felt good, and I was able to release some built-up stress. I thought I'd been treated, but the moment I was discharged, I bought a six-pack of beer. I drove myself and my six-pack from West Palm Beach back to Tampa. I felt so good, I thought I could handle the six-pack without a problem.

But before I even made it home from treatment, I already had an ounce of cocaine on me.

See, this is the problem with bipolar. When you feel good, you're on top of the world. You don't want to take your meds or anything else. You feel like Superman—like you can handle anything life throws at you. And that is a slippery slope. I thought I was maintaining, but I wasn't fooling anybody.

Then my father had a second heart attack. Losing my father was my biggest fear. I'd already lost my mom, my cousin, and my uncle. The last thing I wanted was to lose my father. I went to the hospital and saw my dad. He looked good, given the situation, which was strange. We spoke, but minimally as he was under mild sedation. Still, the situation warranted a drink. I decided I was going to get hammered, which was exactly what I did. I then got pulled over for being intoxicated behind the wheel. I didn't have any weapons on me at the time—only some alcohol, thank goodness.

That last arrest did it for me. They impounded my truck, so my cousin came and saved me. I refused to consent to a breathalyzer test and had my license automatically suspended for a year, based on Florida law.

I was also hit with 60 hours of community service and had to fill out a form known as a FR44. This form skyrocketed my insurance to $600 a month. At least I didn't have to pay my insurance until I reinstated my license. I couldn't apply for a hardship condition because I didn't have a job. I threw my hands to the heavens and pleaded, *"Help me change! I need to turn my life around. I can't keep living in this vicious cycle."* A voice in my head responded, *"Why don't you give back?"*

So, I started volunteering at a food shelter, court ordered at first, prepping meals for those who were less fortunate. In doing that, I came across a certain food store. The manager of the store took a liking to me because he saw me constantly. His store dealt with high-end products and gourmet spices. I told him about my situation and how I'd received a DUI. His response was, "It happens to the best of us."

I asked him what it took to work for him. He asked if I had ever cut meat; I lied and said that I had. Their volume was much different than that of a restaurant, however. Restaurants don't have to break down the meat to the capacity that his store did. I wanted to work for him so I could learn that skillset. I believed that would help me in the future.

He gave me a shot. Me being the ingenious person that I was, I watched a 24-hour crash course on meat cutting on YouTube. He gave me the option to come in the following day and take a meat test. If I passed, I'd have a job that started at $17 an hour. I thought this was my answer to everything. I thought I could see the light at the end of the tunnel. Well, sure enough, I passed the test, thanks to my YouTube education. The bad part was that as soon as I got in there, everyone was doing cocaine.

It only took a minute before I was using cocaine again myself. It seemed that when that white stuff was around, I just couldn't control myself. It got super bad, to where one night, I partied with one of the guys from work and we got so messed up that I couldn't drive. I should have called a cab to get home, but I didn't.

I was walking home and just came to tears. I wanted all of it to stop. I was in one of my low points again and didn't know how to control myself. Once again, I felt that everyone would be better off without me. I still had a pocket knife on me from work, so I just sat on the curb and proceeded to slit my wrist open.

I didn't want my son to ever see his father like this. I looked up to the sky and all I could see was his face. Next thing I knew, I looked down and there was blood gushing out of my veins and going everywhere. I went to call 911, but there was a cop already in the parking lot. He drove around to me and summoned an ambulance, which took me to the hospital. They called my wife and told her what happened. I got Baker Acted *again*, spent the three days in holding, and then was released.

After my release, like tradition, I grabbed the first thing on my mind—more cocaine. That first hit released so much. It was the only way I knew how to cope.

While out under the cover of night, I bought as much cocaine as I could. I had so much cocaine on me, I was delirious. I called my therapist and said I couldn't handle everything. I reached my breaking point again. I couldn't kill myself and was trying to overdose. Again, they called 911, looking for me, but I couldn't figure out where I was. I wandered home and a good friend of mine came over to check on me because he hadn't heard from me in a long time.

He said, "Man, you are going to rehab today!"

I said, "Okay, let's go." And I did. I went to rehab and lived 60 days clean. After those 60 days, the rehab program (number four at this point) sent me to a halfway house. I didn't know what to do in this in-between situation designed to integrate addicts back into society. I was clean, but I wasn't on the best terms with my wife. We still spoke after she left and she let me see my son from time to time; she was good about that. I was down in West Palm Beach, where I didn't know anybody. Inside the halfway house, I wondered, *"How am I supposed to do this?"*

Down in West Palm Beach, my curse was about to rear its ugly head again. After my buy, my phone suddenly rang. It was my dear friend Ghost from college, asking me what I was doing. I told him I let my mind get the best of me again and was about to go back out. He said he'd taught me better than that and added that I shouldn't call him back until I got clean. Then he hung up on me. That last conversation with him was the last time I had a sip of alcohol or used cocaine—four years ago.

COREY HALL

CHAPTER 7
LIFE AFTER REHAB

I got into another treatment center. Keep in mind, I'd already done 60 days at my fourth program. This new program was number five and now I started over from day one. I stayed down in West Palm Beach for a year. By that time, I was in a better position to where I flew home to Tampa on the weekends to spend time with my son. I was doing much better. Being back in the weight room helped, as did taking my medicine and attending intensive therapy. This new program wanted to put me in another halfway house. I told them that didn't work too well for me before. Since they thought I was doing well enough, I was moved to an executive house. That was designed for people who had multiple years of clean time or positive examples of what to do during recovery.

The whole time I was in treatment, I cooked for everybody. My mind went into business mode. If I could get food and money together, I could buy everything at a fraction of the price and break it down myself. I knew about cooking and cleanliness, various ways to prep food, and how to cook at the proper temperature. I decided I wanted to be a private chef. I had cooked and held the position of chef in various restaurants and at the high-end grocery store. The high-end grocery store manager had actually held my job for me because he knew I was in treatment. Out of all the trauma I endured, I started tracking everything. I tracked my entire day. I still do that to this day so I can reference it.

I flew home regularly to avoid staying in Tampa and to avoid the bad influences that triggered my addictions. I stopped drinking completely. However, the rehab center wouldn't let me stay in treatment because I stopped taking all of my medications against medical advice (AMA). One of the medications made me feel sick and I developed stomach ulcers. Since I couldn't stay, the rehab contact had told me, "We're going to give you a little bit more responsibility by letting you start managing houses."

By this time, I was 18 months clean. Still, I decided to stay down in West Palm Beach to hold my position. I didn't have to pay rent and was able to save enough money to pay off my truck and pay back my wife. Since I carried an FR44 form for three years, I paid $600 a month during that time, even for the truck I couldn't drive.

Now that I'm on the other side of the fence, I'm helping people in need. I'm still working and I'm doing my private cooking on the side. It started off slow, but I met people—in the weight room, for example—who opened up networking opportunities. My brother was successful. Over time, my name lost its mark. I got myself physically better and had money in my pocket. Now, I've got established rehab facilities writing me letters of reference and I'm cooking as a private chef for high-end individuals. I've also returned to the Masonic order. One of my good fraternity brothers gave me a road bike to help me lose weight, and I ride that bike every day. Right out of the gate, he and I started riding 20 miles. I weighed around 300 pounds at the time, but I kept working hard. I awoke at 5:00 a.m., did my road work, came back to my meetings, went to work, then came back and worked out.

I learned that you have to find a baseline—some type of stability. Recognize that, or have somebody recognize it for you if you can't. Point it out, stick to it, and build on it. You have to crawl before you can walk, so find out what you like to do. Find out what brings you joy through trial and error. Find what's going to get you out of bed every day and work toward it.

I kept things simple. I got up early, worked out, and wrote everything down. I don't remember things as clearly as I used to, so writing notes ensures I don't forget anything. I've found out what brings me joy, and I work toward that every day. Now, I understand that not everybody has that luxury.

I used to be very creative about getting what I wanted. Now, if I stop being negative and apply that to what will get my family back and bring me happiness every day, then it can work. My journey is not the next man's journey.

The ultimate goal is to get from point A to point B, however it works best for you. My point is that your way may not work for me, and vice-versa.

The first thing you have to do is stop clouding your judgment with drugs and/or alcohol. I know they seem like they work and help ease the pain. False. They drain your money, create more problems, and stall any progress.

What did my alcohol abuse cost me? For starters, I don't have access to my son or my wife. That was one major sacrifice. I also gave up what I thought made me happy. I had to focus on responsibility—anything to help build my future. Going out and drinking wasn't doing it. Staying up late wasn't doing it. I had to K.I.S.S.—keep it simple, stupid. Build from the nucleus out. When you are the nucleus, everything starts with you, and it starts with the way you think, the way you act, the way you move, the way you dress and how you carry yourself.

Be advised, I'm not saying it's guaranteed to happen. I had to sacrifice my family and my livelihood. I lost my mom; I lost my cousin; I lost my uncle. I've suffered enough to where either I could stay down or make a change. I chose to become someone who put himself in a position to write a book with a great publishing company, live his dream, make money, be on TV, and fly around the world, doing what he loves doing. That all started with just a dream. But it's only worth it if you work toward it and don't shoot yourself in the foot by making dumb decisions. You have to consciously think and play the tape through, asking: *"Is this going to advance me? Is it going to keep me where I am, or is it going to set me back?"*

Nobody's going to do it for you. Nobody's going to get you up at 5:00 a.m. The reason why I love waking up at 5:00 a.m. is that I'm working harder than my addiction and my insecurities. I've redeveloped a work ethic that was once in place. I believe in something greater than me, and my goal is to make sure my son knows I didn't die on my knees. I chose to live on my feet and to fight.

Setbacks happen. I always say to myself, *"You can't do epic shit with basic people."* Therefore, I don't surround myself with anyone doing less than me. That's hard to do, because as one of my therapists told me, "Your one hundred percent is not someone else's one hundred percent." Still, I would rather do it slower by myself than not have it done right. I believe in quality over quantity. I try to be as righteous as I can, and I'm a perfect example of imperfection. I'm all right if I die tomorrow because I've done everything I could with the time I had today.

THANK YOU FOR TAKING THE TIME TO HELP ME…

SEE IT THROUGH.

COREY HALL

EPILOGUE: ABOUT BIPOLAR DISORDER

Definition

According to the National Institute of Mental Health, bipolar disorder (sometimes also called manic depression) causes abrupt shifts in focus, energy, activity, and mood.

The Mayo Clinic lists the following as just some of the possible symptoms of bipolar disorder:

- Abnormally upbeat, jumpy, or wired

- Increased activity or agitation

- Exaggerated sense of well-being and self-confidence

- Unusual talkativeness

- Racing thoughts

- Poor decision-making (such as impulsive buying sprees, for instance)

Manic Episodes

Typically, people with bipolar have a tendency to be extremely "up" (manic episodes), where they're absolutely wired, bouncing off the walls with energy.

From the outside looking in, a manic episode looks like erratic behavior, and it is. You don't eat. Sometimes you don't sleep. You have irrational thoughts and find yourself doing things that you wouldn't be doing while on the medication. You may not eat, shower, shave, or take care of yourself in other ways.

During the manic episodes, if you have children, your brain turns caring for them into solving a quadratic equation. Your mind is racing, you have no control of it, and you can't stop it. So you have no idea how to put the formula together to make it work.

You can't compartmentalize or organize yourself to where you have to have an order of operation where you can take care of the most important to the least important. It just becomes one big puddle of mud. Of course, it puts a huge strain on personal relationships. It doesn't matter if you're rich or poor, if you come from a good upbringing or a bad one—bipolar disorder's effects don't discriminate.

It's an invisible monster, in my opinion, that you definitely need help with if you want to conquer it.

Depressive Episodes

After the manic episode comes the "crash" (depressive episodes). The elation of the manic episode is replaced with depression, to where you may sleep for days. Once again, you may not be showering, eating, etc., but this time it's because you have no energy. You feel totally depressed and hopeless.

People with bipolar have a tendency to self-medicate with drugs (like weed or pills) or alcohol, for instance. Substances like this can take your mind off of the issues you're having and temporarily allow you to cope. However, that's just adding to your problem. Now, not only do you have a medical disability, but you have a substance abuse problem, which also has to be dealt with.

Bipolar has many different faces. There are different types, such as type one and type two, and therefore there's not a black-and-white bipolar medication that specifically targets the problem. It's sort of a hit-or-miss based on your height, weight, age, and sex as you figure out the right combination for your personal condition. You have to at least give each medication a chance and take it for 30 to 90 days to see if it stabilizes your system.

Most people I know with bipolar have a tendency, once they start to feel better, to think that they can manage the situation without the medications. But that then puts you back to where you were in the beginning, where something can come out of nowhere and suck all of the energy out of your body because it's the only thing you can focus on.

I haven't had an episode in almost four years now, at least not knowingly, because of the coping skills that I obtained when I was in treatment. One of those is eliminating any potential triggers. Every day, you have to work on that. Some people think, *"I don't have bipolar today. I feel good,"* which has not been the case in my experience. I'll never say that.

You have to ask for help until you have a routine to where you can do it without being told you can, without even thinking about it, kind of like breathing. It has to be like an instinct.

At one point, I was almost up to 310 pounds on all the different medications. I stopped all the drugs and all the drinking, but the medications I was on had caused an ulcer. At the treatment facility, they said I couldn't stay there if I wasn't on medications. They also insisted that I had to have surgery to where they were going to cut out some of my stomach. I said no.

The thing is, when you enter an in-patient facility, you've got to accept the process, abide by their rules, and do what they say, and when they say it. You can't rebut any of that until you know what you're talking about. That means that you have to experience and accept it to the point where you can make an informed decision on what you want to do differently. But it's not just what you want to do, it's how you're going to get there and what steps you're going to take. If you don't do what they initially advise, you're not going to know what does and doesn't work. Just because you don't like it doesn't mean it's not going to work for you.

I did the 12 steps. One day, I stood up in class and basically told them that the steps weren't working for me. They told me,

"Well, it's your program," so I adapted things accordingly. I could only do that because I didn't have any write-ups. I wasn't a problem child. I applied myself and relied on the experiences and things I'd accomplished before I ever had bipolar episodes or experimented with drugs.

I'd once been told I couldn't play Division I football, and I did it anyway. I'd been told I couldn't be elite in the military, but I did that, too—even though my bipolar had started at that time, and I only accomplished that through work. So, that was why I went against medical advice and decided to help myself with just work and exercise, which I was accustomed to because of football and the military.

I changed everything from the way I thought, to my diet, and even the people I hung around with. It was the little things at first, minor details like getting up and making my bed first, and I built on those. I was sick and tired of being sick and tired, and I worked toward changing it.

Basically, you have to have a foundation, something solid that you can fall back on. Sometimes it's family, sometimes it's a higher power, but either way, you've got to work on it every day.

I discovered what worked for me, and I've stuck with it ever since. To deviate from my norm isn't a good idea, and I know that. I have to take steps and have boundaries and milestones to achieve personal goals. I don't try to achieve those overnight anymore because I know where that leads.

Someone gave me an explanation that because I'd been using drugs and self-medicating for over 10 years, it would take me about that long to completely relearn a better way of living. I did it in about two years, just because that was what I stuck to every day when I woke up and every night when I went to sleep. It was just what I had to do.

In terms of personal relationships, loved ones are bad about enabling people with bipolar disorder. I mean, that's a big problem. Nobody wants to see someone they care about in pain. So, you might try to help someone out by giving them a couple dollars, maybe so they don't go do something illegal.

Unfortunately, that's probably the worst thing you can do. People get used to that and start to take advantage. They become cunning and think of ingenious ways to manipulate situations that benefit them, which is what I did.

Enabling doesn't help anyone. It makes the person with bipolar that much worse. And eventually, the enabler gets fed up to the point where they no longer care what happens. So, then you revert back to your feral ways and use any means necessary to stop the pain.

If you have an inkling that a loved one needs help, don't wait. Al-Anon is just like an Alcoholics Anonymous group, but for the family members of narcotic addicts. It teaches loved ones to cope with a person, whether the person has problems with substance abuse or mental health. In Al-Anon meetings, you'll meet people going through what you are, and you might hear something that you've noticed, but you didn't know what to call it.

If you have a loved one who is suffering from something and you're really not sure what it is, do a urine analysis. You can buy it from any drugstore. That'll give you a baseline. What's going to happen from there is that the person will either fight the issue and make excuses, or they'll take the test.

If they fight you, you know there's an issue, because if you give somebody with nothing to hide a urine analysis, they'll say, "Yeah, I'll go do it." But don't be naïve and just give them the bottle.

I've worked in treatment centers where people would cheat the test—because if your time in the facility is court-ordered and you violate a urine analysis, you're going to jail—and the people in the hierarchy really didn't care. As long as the tests were clean, they were getting money, for the most part.

There are different kinds of treatment facilities. A 30-day house, for instance, requires people to go through intensive treatment and therapy. Then you have outpatient treatment, halfway houses, and things of that nature. That's what everybody wants to get to because then you have a little bit of freedom. But in those places, you'll have housemates who are also in recovery.

I was at a lot of treatment centers where program graduates got free residence and took charge of the houses. So, it was kind of like the blind leading the blind. Accountability was therefore almost zero. If someone gets to stay at a facility for free and his only job is to collect rent and do the urine analysis, so long as the samples come back clean, they don't really care where they come from.

You might wonder what the point of such places is, if there's no accountability. But the point of being there is that you're not in the environment from where you came. You still have the protection of the group because there's a group almost every day, every hour that you can attend.

The reason I know so much about it is because I went to five or six different treatment centers over my bout. I was in charge of a lot of houses and I did a lot of volunteer work. So, I was in it from every angle there is.

The last treatment center I attended, I'd already been clean for over a year, but I was awarded the opportunity to stay there for free, which meant I would be removed from the element that I was having issues with and would also get paid by the treatment centers to watch the houses.

I also got to volunteer for them because I was doing my cooking. So, I was there for almost a year and a half. I'm still married, and at the time, I would fly back from West Palm to Tampa every chance I got.

However, as my wife is from London, she obviously got lonely with just her and our son living alone. Therefore, I had to let my wife go back to England and take our son with her.

I've been fighting this beast for 10 years. It hurt me, because I thought I was doing the right thing. I was thinking everything was great, but you don't always take into account the pain that the person on the other end of bipolar is experiencing. So, in order for me to get right, I had to let some things go.

My man Tone from P-Townfunk told me, "If you don't let those things go, nobody's going to get better. You're going to be constantly fighting something that you can't control, which is not going to help you, and she's not going to get any better, because she can't help herself."

It's been the most painful thing, seeing my son grow up over Skype, but he's getting one of the best educations at a private school in London, and my wife has her family with her. I get to see him every three months when he's not at school. That's just a necessary evil that I have to accept. If I don't accept it, I can't move forward, and nobody wins.

My mother died from bipolar disorder. My cousin committed suicide; my uncle committed suicide. Bipolar killed a lot of people in my family and is still affecting us to this day. So, sometimes you've just got to cut some things loose and say, "Fuck it."

You can only fight what you can control. If I'm not happy, I can't make anybody else happy. That's just something you've got to accept.

ABOUT THE AUTHOR

Chef Corey Hall resides in sunny Florida with his father. He is utilizing his culinary skills to cook for the stars. He frequents Los Angeles to see his brother, Pooch Hall, who is starring on the famous Showtime series *Ray Donovan*.

Corey flies to London as much as possible to see his son and still strives be a part of his life as much as possible.

He has also started a company to help kids with health and nutrition to get them into shape.

Follow Corey on Instagram to keep up with his progress: @TruChef8384 and @ech_culinary_artistry

www.ingramcontent.com/pod-product-compliance
Lightning Source LLC
Chambersburg PA
CBHW060042230426
43661CB00004B/628